P9-CFT-113

Discovering Cultures

Argentina

Sharon Gordon

MARSHALL CAVENDISH
NEW YORK

With thanks to Peter T. Johnson, Princeton University, for the careful review of this manuscript.

Benchmark Books
Marshall Cavendish
99 White Plains Road
Tarrytown, New York 10591-9001
www.marshallcavendish.com

Text copyright © 2004 by Marshall Cavendish Corporation
Map and illustrations copyright © 2004 by Marshall Cavendish Corporation

All rights reserved. No part of this book may be reproduced or utilized in any form or by any means electronic or mechanical, including photocopying, recording, or by any information storage and retrieval system, without written permission from the copyright holders.

All Internet sites were available and accurate when sent to press.

Library of Congress Cataloging-in-Publication Data

Gordon, Sharon.
Argentina / by Sharon Gordon.
p. cm. — (Discovering cultures)
Summary: An introduction to the geography, history, people, and culture of Argentina.
Includes bibliographical references and index.
ISBN 0-7614-1723-0
1. Argentina—Juvenile literature. [1. Argentina.] I. Title. II. Series.
F2808.2.G67 2003
982—dc22   2003019097

Photo Research by Candlepants Incorporated

Cover Photo: Sergio Pitamitz/Corbis

The photographs in this book are used by permission and through the courtesy of; *Getty Images*: Terry Vine, back cover; Chad Ehlers, 9, 42 (right); Robert Van Der Hilst, 18; Scott Markewitz, 30. *Corbis*: 4, 13, 42 (left), 43 (center); Pablo Corral Vega, 1, 8, 14, 15, 25, 26; Craig Lovell, 6-7, 43 (bottom); Yann Arthus-Bertrand, 10; Hubert Stadler, 16; Caroline Penn, 24; Simon Bruty/SI/NewSport, 28 (bottom); Owen Franken, 28 (top), 31; Kit Houghton, 29; Bettmann 44 (both); Najlah Feanny/SABA, 45. *Robert Fried*: 11, 12, 19, 20, 42 (bottom). *Envision*: Osentoski& Zoda, 21; Steven Needham, 22. ©*Comasana*: Francisco Pontoriero/Fotoscopio, 32; Claudio Suter/Fotoscopio, 34-35; Fernando Calzada/Fotoscopio, 36 (top & bottom). *Blaine Harrington III*: 37, 38.

Cover: *Casa Rosada, Buenos Aires, Argentina*; Title page: *Playful children in Buenos Aires*

Map and illustrations by Ian Warpole
Book design by Virginia Pope

Printed in China
1 3 5 6 4 2

Turn the Pages...

Where in the World Is Argentina?

Argentina is the second-largest country in South America. It is a long nation on the eastern coast, stretching 2,300 miles (3,701 kilometers) from north to south. It is part of the "tail" of South America. Argentina is about one-third the size of the United States. Chile and the Andes Mountains form its western border. On the north and east are Bolivia, Paraguay, Brazil, Uruguay, and the stormy Atlantic Ocean. The name *Argentina* means "silver." The Spanish who came here hoped to find a lot of this valuable metal, just as they had in other areas of the Andes.

Mount Aconcagua is the highest peak in the Americas.

Map of Argentina

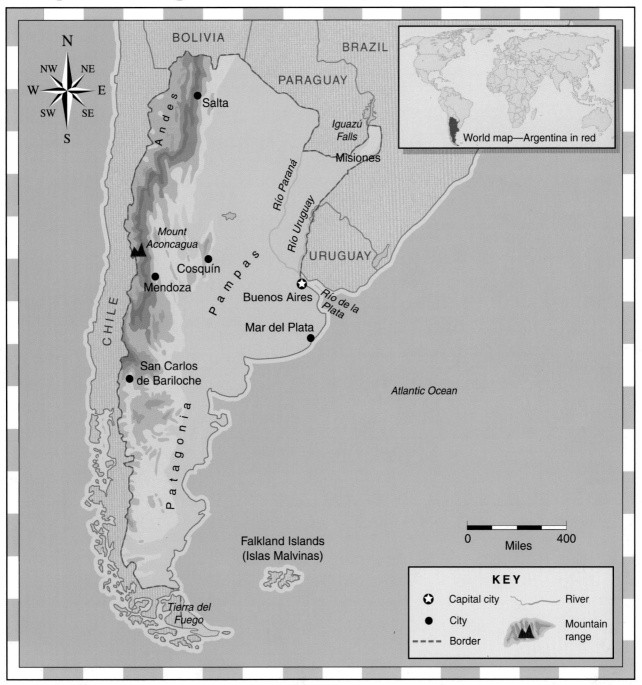

BOLIVIA

BRAZIL

PARAGUAY

N
NW NE
W E
SW SE
S

Andes

Salta

Iguazú Falls

Misiones

Río Paraná

Río Uruguay

URUGUAY

Mount Aconcagua

P a m p a s

Cosquín

Mendoza

Buenos Aires

Río de la Plata

Mar del Plata

CHILE

San Carlos de Bariloche

P a t a g o n i a

Atlantic Ocean

World map—Argentina in red

Falkland Islands (Islas Malvinas)

0 — Miles — 400

Tierra del Fuego

KEY

☆ Capital city	River
● City	Mountain range
- - - - Border	

Argentina is a land of great contrasts in land, people, and weather. The highest peak in the Americas is found in Argentina in the Andes Mountains. Mount Aconcagua is 22,831 feet (6,959 meters) high. The climate in the northern Andes is dry and dusty. The southern Andes are rainy and wooded. The peaks of the mountains are always white with snow. Tourists come to Mount Tronador (the thunderer) to hear the great cracking noise that is made when large chunks of ice melt in the summer.

Large, flat plains called *pampas* cover an area of almost 1,000 miles (1,609 km) in the center of Argentina. The word *pampa* means "level plain." Crops such as wheat, soybeans, sunflowers, and corn are grown here. The pampas also have many large cattle ranches called *estancias* that are known for their fine beef. These ranches are home to Argentine cowboys called *gauchos*.

The pampas in central Argentina

Buenos Aires at night

With so much land to graze on, the cattle do not have to eat hay or oats. They produce delicious, lean meat.

Buenos Aires is the capital of Argentina. Its name means "good winds." It is located on the banks of the Río de la Plata. Most of the country's industries, businesses, and government offices are located in this modern city. Buenos Aires is known for its wide, tree-lined streets. It is also an important seaport. Residents of Buenos Aires are called "Porteños," or people of the port.

Avenida 9 de Julio is the widest street in the world.

Many streets in Argentina's major cities are named after important events in the country's history. Avenida 9 de Julio (Avenue of July 9) in Buenos Aires is named after the date that Argentina became an independent nation. It is 460 feet (140 m) wide, the widest street in the world.

In the south, flat, dry lands called Patagonia cover one-quarter of Argentina. Not many people live here. Off the southern tip of the country is the island of Tierra del Fuego, which means "land of fire." It was named by the Spanish when they saw the campfires of the Indians. Argentina shares this windy island with Chile.

An empty area of Patagonia

Off the east coast lie the Falkland Islands, which are claimed by both Great Britain and Argentina. The Argentines call them the Islas Malvinas. When Argentina became an independent nation in 1816, it claimed these islands. But the British took them back, and have controlled them ever since.

In the northeast there is an area of rich farmland called Mesopotamia. It lies between two rivers, the Uruguay and the Paraná. The Paraná is the second-longest river in South America. In northern Mesopotamia is Misiones, a *province* of forests and *savannas*. It was named after the missions set up by Catholic priests in the 1630s. One of the most fantastic sights in South America, the thundering Iguazú Falls, is found here.

The Iguazú Falls

In the northwest corner of the province of Misiones are the amazing Iguazú Falls. Two hundred seventy-five different waterfalls make up the falls. Iguazú means "great waters" in the native Guaraní language. The horseshoe-shaped falls are located on the border of Brazil and Argentina. Two-thirds of the falls are on the Argentine side. The Iguazú Falls are taller than Niagara Falls and four times as wide. Falls like "Garganta del Diablo" (devil's throat) spray water high in the air. They produce large, bright rainbows in the sky. The tumbling water drops 240 feet (73 m) to the Iguazú River. Visitors can take boat rides under the powerful falls. They can walk along paths that offer amazing views. Iguazú is surrounded by national parks on both the Argentine and the Brazilian side of the border.

What Makes Argentina Argentine?

Most Argentines have European ancestors. They think of themselves as being more European than South American. For hundreds of years, the country was controlled by Spain. Spanish is still the official language. In the late 1800s, many Italians came to Argentina looking for construction work. Today, they are the largest group in Argentina. There are also French, German, Swiss, British, Bolivian, Peruvian, and Korean residents. Indians make up only 1 percent of the population. A mixture of Indians and Europeans, called mestizos, make up another 14 percent.

Many Argentines have European backgrounds.

The president of Argentina lives in the Casa Rosada.

The Republic of Argentina has a constitution similar to that of the United States. The president leads the government. He is helped by a council of ministers. The president lives in the Casa Rosada, or the Pink House, in Buenos Aires. The color pink was chosen in 1873 to represent two political groups—red for the federals and white for the unitarians. Like the United States, Argentina also has a national congress that passes new laws.

Until its independence from Spain, Argentina's artistic style came from Europe. Many Argentines went to school in Europe. When they returned to Argentina, they brought European art, music, and architecture with them. Buenos Aires has many important art museums and theaters. The National Fine Arts

Teatro Colon is one of the world's best opera houses.

Museum, in the Recoleta district, has many famous European paintings from artists like Renoir and Monet.

Argentines enjoy all kinds of music. Teatro Colon, also in Buenos Aires, is one of the greatest opera houses in the world. The elaborate building holds 2,500 seats and is known for its excellent acoustics. It was designed by Francisco Tamburri, an Italian architect. Before each new performance, craftsmen hand-paint the huge backdrop. Over the years, many internationally known opera stars have come here to sing.

The folk music of Argentina comes from both the Europeans and the Indians. Creole music is a blend of Spanish and local cultures. The *zamba* is the national dance of Argentina, and the *gato* is the most important rural dance. Couples enjoy these dances on many holidays, especially Carnival. The *escondido* is the dance of the gauchos. Its music sounds like galloping horses.

Many of Argentina's artists and writers have lived in difficult times. Those who fought for independence from Spain were treated badly. They were threatened by the military powers or by local warlords called *caudillos*. From 1976 to 1983, the military ruled Argentina during a time called the Dirty War. Thousands of people who were against the military disappeared during the Dirty War. Many were women and children. Today, women's rights workers are still trying to find out what happened to the missing children.

Argentine families are very close. A typical Argentine household will have grandparents, parents, and children all living under the same roof. When children get married, they often live near their parents. More and more women are entering the workforce to help support their families.

Because of its strong ties to Spain and Italy, most Argentines are Roman Catholic. However, the second-largest Jewish community in the Americas lives mainly in Buenos Aires. According to the law, the president and vice president of Argentina must be Catholics.

Nothing is more Argentine than the tradition of the gauchos. In the 1800s, these rugged cowboys rode across the vast pampas, looking

A gaucho in traditional clothing

Cowboys at the Gaucho National Festival

for cattle or wild horses. They wore wide-brimmed hats and baggy pants called *bombachas*. They used a weapon called a *boleadora*, made of three stones on a leather strap. The gauchos threw the boleadora at their target.

Today, some of these cowboys still live their simple lifestyle in the pampas. In the summer, many horse-riding fans attend the annual Gaucho National Festival in San Antonio de Areco. Men and women perform traditional dances and dress in colorful costumes. Many gauchos still use the old saddles that were used by their grandfathers.

The Tango

The tango is both a kind of music and a dance. The tango started in the poor areas of Buenos Aires in the early 1900s and spread throughout the country. The slow, sad music usually speaks about lost loves or the troubles of life. Tango dancers take long steps together as they glide gracefully along the floor. They must have perfect timing. Learning to tango is popular in the United States, too. Many tango dance competitions can be seen on television.

Living in Argentina

Argentina is in the southern *hemisphere* of the world. Because of this, its seasons are exactly the opposite of the United States. January and February are the hottest summer months. Schools are out, and January is the most popular time for vacation. Work slows down. Families have time to travel and visit other areas of the country.

Argentines may work in banks, factories, or hospitals. Some have jobs in construction, or building. Others work for the government. Farming is very important,

A rancher herds his sheep.

Life in the city is busy.

especially in the rich soil of the pampas. Wheat, corn, and other grains are grown for sale in Argentina, as well as in other countries. Vineyards in the province of Mendoza grow grapes for making wine and olive trees for making olive oil.

Eight out of ten Argentines live in cities. Most city dwellers live in or near Buenos Aires. Life in the city is modern and fast. Shopping and dining out are favorite weekend activities. City people stay up late and enjoy the exciting nightlife. But the farmers and ranchers living in the countryside work long days and go to bed early. They do not feel they have much in common with the people living in Buenos Aires.

Colorful homes

In 2001, Argentina suffered from a banking crisis. People could not use their savings and many businesses had to close. In a two-week period, Argentina had five different presidents. Many people lost their jobs. At the same time, the price of food went up. Many people became homeless and hungry. They went into the streets to protest, banging pots and pans together. The crisis left over half of the population in poverty, unable to afford food or clothing. Today, the government is working to improve conditions for these people.

Buenos Aires is divided into many areas called *barrios*. Each barrio is different. Along the docks on the waterfront is a barrio called La Boca (the mouth). It has homes made of materials from old ships. Many are tin and painted in bright colors. La Boca is famous because it is the home of the tango. In the Recoleta barrio, there is one of the most expensive cemeteries in the world. Many visitors come to see the graves that have fancy monuments. Only the very rich can afford to be buried here.

Argentines start their day with a simple breakfast, such as a roll and a cup of coffee. Around 1:30 P.M., they have a big meal. Sometimes, they take a nap in the heat of the day until 3:00 P.M. or 4:00 P.M., and then go back to work. Some businesses stay open until 8:00 P.M. or 9:00 P.M. Government offices close between 2:00 P.M. and 6:00 P.M.

After work, Argentines may go out to visit friends and family. They have their last meal of the day after nine o'clock at night. They enjoy going out to dinner, which can last for hours. Since so many people are of Italian heritage,

Ingredients for a tasty chicken dish

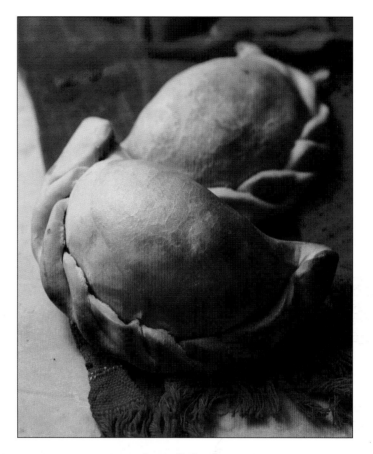

Empanadas stuffed with meat

pizza and pasta are very popular. So is Italian ice cream, which is called *helado*. Since Argentines eat dinner so late, many restaurants stay open until after midnight.

Argentines eat large amounts of beef each year. Delicious beef from the local ranches is usually served twice a day. It is said that the average Argentine eats 154 pounds (70 kilograms) of beef each year! Popular dishes are spicy sausages called *chorizos*, meat-stuffed pastries called *empanadas*, and *locro*, a tasty corn stew. After church on Sundays, families may leave the city and go into the country for an *asado*, an outdoor barbecue.

Let's Eat!
Empanadas

Empanadas, or beef pies, are popular throughout Argentina. Ask an adult to help you prepare this recipe.

Ingredients:

4 cups unbleached flour

4 tablespoons vegetable shortening

1/2 tablespoon salt

2 onions

1 green bell pepper

1/2 pound lean steak, cut into small pieces

1/3 cup seedless raisins

1/4 cup green olives, finely chopped

1 bunch green onions, minced

1 hard-boiled egg, minced

paprika

salt

crushed red pepper

Wash your hands. In a medium-size frying pan, melt two tablespoons vegetable shortening. Dice the onion and bell pepper. Add to the pan. Cook over medium heat until the onion turns golden. Add the diced meat. Season to taste with salt, red pepper, and paprika. Cook, stirring occasionally, until the beef turns brown on all sides. Remove the frying pan from the heat. Mix in the egg, the raisins, the olives, and the green onions. Allow to cool to room temperature.

Pour the flour on a smooth surface, forming a mound. Using the back of a spoon, make a dent in the center. Put three tablespoons shortening in the dent. Knead the ingredients until fully mixed. Fill a cup with warm water and dissolve the salt. Gradually mix this liquid into the dough, kneading 10–15 minutes until the dough becomes smooth and elastic.

Pull off balls of dough about the size of a golf ball. On the floured surface, roll out each ball of dough into a four-inch circle. Flour your hands. Hold the dough circle in one hand and place one tablespoon of the filling in the center. Press and crimp the edges of the dough together. Preheat oven to 450 degrees Fahrenheit (232 degrees Celsius). Lightly flour a baking sheet. Arrange the empanadas on the sheet and bake until the pastry is golden brown, about ten minutes.

School Days

Argentina has a very high literacy rate. That means most people in the country can read and write. Although the government of Argentina supports education, local provinces pay for their own schools.

The school year runs from March to November. Students must go to school for nine years. All children between the ages of six and fourteen must attend school. Grades ten through twelve are not

High school students show their work to their teacher.

required. Some children go to school in the morning, starting at 8:00 A.M. Others go after lunch. When students arrive at school, they put up the flag and sing the national anthem.

Most students attend state schools, which are free and not religious. Some parents pay for their children to go to private schools. Many schools have some kind of uniform. Both students and teachers often wear simple white coats. There are no public school buses and students must buy their own books and

A classroom in Buenos Aires

uniforms. In rural areas, some children go to school on horseback. Some ranches have a one-room schoolhouse for children whose parents live and work there.

Almost half of all Argentine students attend secondary school, or high school. Students study the same subjects at each level throughout the country. There is a basic level and a higher level. In the higher level, students take classes that fit their future goals, such as farming or acting.

An art student makes a clay figure.

Over 40 percent of high school graduates go on to a college or university. Most universities are free and open to everyone. The University of Buenos Aires is one of the oldest in Argentina. It has a good reputation in science and technology and has produced five Nobel Prize winners.

Most Argentine students learn to speak English and French in school, since they are important international languages. The Spanish spoken in Argentina is called Castilian. It comes from Castile, Spain. Since there are Italian Argentines, Italian words are often mixed in with the Spanish. Lunfardo mixes Spanish and Italian. It is spoken mainly in Buenos Aires.

The Child Journalist Project

The Child Journalist Project began ten years ago in the poor neighborhoods of Buenos Aires. The program helps children learn to be better writers and speakers. It also helps them to learn to become young reporters. First, they pick a topic, such as disappearing trees or the rights of children. Then they interview people on the street who are affected by the problem. They write reports and talk about them in class. They decide how to present their news stories. Some stories become newspaper articles, videos, or radio programs. Students use tape recorders and cameras to help them cover a story. Their stories are aired in the schools and in the community.

Just for Fun

By far, the most popular Argentine sport is *fútbol* (soccer). It was brought to Argentina by British sailors in the 1840s. Young children take the game seriously as they play in the streets. Many dream of playing with the Boca Juniors or River Plate, two of Argentina's professional teams. Argentine players are known for their skill in handling the ball. Argentina's national team has won the World Cup twice, in 1978 and 1986. Both times, there were great street celebrations in Buenos Aires.

A boy heads a soccer ball.

Argentines compete in a World Cup soccer match.

Polo is a popular sport in Argentina.

From the gauchos, Argentines have developed a love of horses. Many of their sports involve riding horses. Horseback riding is very popular, especially among the descendants of the original gauchos. Rodeos are popular. There, skilled riders participate in competitions. Show jumping is another exciting event.

Polo, brought to Argentina by British immigrants, is also a popular horse sport. In fact, Argentina has some of the best polo players and ponies in the world. Players riding on ponies try to move a wooden ball across a field and into the goal. They use *mallets* to hit the ball. There are four players on each team. The six play periods that make up the ninety-minute match are called chukkers. Children learn to play polo by swinging mallets while riding their bicycles.

The Argentine ski season runs from June to October, but July and August are the best months. Skiers

Skiing in the mountains

and snowboarders can enjoy winter sports at many places, such as Las Leñas Valley in Mendoza and Mount Cathedral in San Carlos de Bariloche.

During the hot summer months, residents from in and around Buenos Aires flock to the beaches. Mar del Plata is one of the most popular. It is about 250 miles (402 km) south of the capital, on the northern Atlantic coast. Along with miles of some of the best beaches in South America, there are beautiful sand dunes, high cliffs, and fishing villages. People enjoy the fresh seafood offered in the area's many restaurants.

The good weather makes cafés popular in Argentina, just as they are in Spain and Italy. Neighbors and friends enjoy sitting at a sidewalk table, having a cup of coffee or soda, and relaxing. Chess is often played in cafés. Over the years, Argentina has produced many world-famous chess players.

Drinking a cup of *yerba maté* with a friend or neighbor is a relaxing pastime. Yerba maté is a type of green tea made from the leaves of the yerba maté tree. Argentines sip it out of a round, wooden cup called a *maté*. It is sipped through a straw called a *bombilla*. The Spanish made matés from silver, wood, or *gourds*. They made bombillas from silver or other metals. Yerba maté was first popular with the gauchos. Its popularity soon spread throughout the country.

Sipping maté from a gourd

Riding the "Train to the Clouds"

Both tourists and native Argentines enjoy riding the "Train to the Clouds." At 13,000 feet (3,962 m), it is one of the three highest trains in the world. It begins in the Andes Mountains and passes through beautiful landscapes. Often, the train is so high in the air that riders can see clouds under the bridges it crosses. It leaves the city of Salta and finally stops at La Polvorilla station, its highest point. The trip takes nearly fifteen hours, and includes thirty-three bridges and twenty-one tunnels.

Pato

The game of pato is played only in Argentina. Two teams of four horseback riders must get a leather ball through a basket at the end of the field. The word *pato* in Spanish means "duck." Unfortunately, when the game began in the early 1600s, players used a real duck instead of a ball. The game was not allowed after 1882 because of this cruelty. However, in 1938, the rules of the game were changed to replace the duck with a leather ball. Pato is now popular again.

Let's Celebrate!

It is believed that the Manca Fiesta (Festival of the Pot) is the oldest festival in Argentina. It is celebrated in the northern town of La Quiaca during the third and fourth Sunday of October. Local Indian crafters put their native pots and pottery on display. They trade them to Argentines and their Bolivian neighbors for clothing or dried meats. Many traders still use llamas and donkeys to carry their goods back and forth to the festival.

Christmas in Argentina comes during the summer month of December. Some people put up evergreen trees and decorate them with cotton balls to look like snow. Christmas Eve is called Noche Buena. Some families sing carols as they go from house to house. Dinner might be eaten outside on the patio or inside the air-conditioned house. Iced tea is enjoyed along with a dinner of roast pork, turkey, or beef. If the weather is nice, families might have a Christmas barbecue or

Fireworks over Mar del Plata

picnic. The children play while the adults talk. Everyone opens presents and waits for the fireworks to begin.

The National Folklore Festival for Argentina is held in Cosquín each January. Folk music is performed by dancers and musicians from all over Argentina. In the outdoor theater, there are performances from ten o'clock in the morning until midnight.

Smaller perform-ances are held throughout the town. Food and drinks are sold to those who are watching. People from all over the world come to Cosquín for this lively celebration.

Folk music fills the air

Argentina is known around the world for its excellent red wines. In February, Mendoza holds a weeklong wine festival called La Fiesta de la Vendimia. It celebrates the end of the grape harvest. The people call their home along the Andes "the land of sun and good wine." The grape vines are blessed by a Catholic priest. Those who attend the festival receive free red wine. A parade is held and a harvest festival queen is chosen. La Fiesta de la Vendimia ends with a large display of fireworks.

In July, crafters display their unique ponchos at the Fiesta del Poncho in Catamarca. A poncho is like a blanket worn over the shoulders with a hole cut in the center for a person's head. Indians first used handwoven ponchos. Now, people enjoy their beauty and warmth. Many women make these beautiful ponchos. Their

Dressed for Carnival

art has been passed down from one generation to the next. The ponchos are made from the wool of the alpaca, llama, sheep, or vicuña. These four animals live high in the Andes Mountains. One poncho can take months to make.

Mar del Plata, on the coast, celebrates the Harvest of Fish with feasts of good seafood. The people of the town dress up as sea creatures and march in a parade. They follow the Queen of the Sea, who leads the parade while sitting in a huge shell.

Many celebrations in Argentina are tied to the Catholic Church. Carnival is a festival celebrated by Catholics around the world. It begins six weeks before Easter. Carnival is celebrated with parades, parties, and delicious food. Each area of the country has a different way of celebrating. In the province of Salta, people dress up and dance the zamba and *carnavalito*. They sing songs and play harps and accordions.

Celebrating Carnival

The Feast of the Epiphany

In many Latin American countries, January 6 is an important holiday for children. It is the day when the Three Kings came from far away to visit the baby Jesus. In Argentina, a nativity scene is placed under the Christmas tree. Each day, the figures of the Three Kings are moved closer and closer to the tree. On the eve of January 6, the kings are placed right next to the baby Jesus. Children place their shoes underneath the Christmas tree or beside their beds. They leave hay and water for the kings' camels. In the morning, the food and water are gone, and presents are found in their shoes instead.

The Argentine flag has three horizontal stripes. The top and bottom stripes are sky blue. The middle stripe is white and features a sun with a face. The colors were chosen by a leader in Argentina's revolution for independence from Spain in 1812.

Argentine money is the peso. Each peso equals 100 centavos, or cents. There are 2, 5, 10, 20, 50, and 100 pesos bills. As of October 2003, 2.81 pesos equaled one U.S. dollar.

Count in Spanish

English	Spanish	Say it like this:
one	uno	OO-noh
two	dos	DOHS
three	tres	TRACE
four	cuatro	KWAH-troh
five	cinco	SEEN-koh
six	seis	SAYSS
seven	siete	see-EH-tay
eight	ocho	OH-choh
nine	nueve	NWEH-beh
ten	diez	dee-EHS

Glossary

barrio (BAR-ee-o)   An area or neighborhood that is unique in style and culture.

gaucho (GOW-choh)   A cowboy from the Argentine pampas.

gourd (GORD)   A large fruit that grows on vines and has a hard outer shell.

hemisphere (HEM-uh-sfeer)   One-half of the surface of the earth.

mallet   A hammerlike, wooden tool that is used to strike a ball.

pampas (POM-pahs)   A large, flat, grass-covered area in Argentina.

poverty   A condition in which a person does not have money, and is very poor.

province   An area of a country; like a state in the U.S.

savanna   An open, flat area without trees.

yerba maté (YER-bah mah-TAY)   A drink made from the leaves of the yerba maté tree.

Fast Facts

Argentina is the second-largest country in South America. It is about one-third the size of the United States.

The highest peak in the Americas is found in Argentina in the Andes Mountains. Mount Aconcagua is 22,831 feet (6,959 m) high.

Buenos Aires is the capital of Argentina. Its name means "good winds." It is located on the banks of the Río de la Plata.

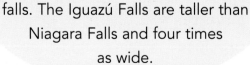

The horseshoe-shaped Iguazú Falls are located on the border of Brazil and Argentina. Two hundred seventy-five different waterfalls make up the falls. The Iguazú Falls are taller than Niagara Falls and four times as wide.

The Argentine flag has three horizontal stripes. The top and bottom stripes are sky blue. The middle stripe is white and features a sun with a face.

In 2003 in Argentina, 92 percent of the people were Roman Catholic, 2 percent were Protestant, 2 percent were Jewish, and 4 percent followed other religions.

Argentine money is the peso. Each peso has 100 centavos, or cents. There are 2, 5, 10, 20, 50, and 100 pesos bills. As of October 2003, 2.81 pesos equaled one U.S. dollar.

The Republic of Argentina has a constitution similar to that of the United States. The president leads the government. He is helped by a council of ministers. Like the United States, Argentina also has a national congress that passes new laws.

Argentina is in the southern hemisphere of the world. Its seasons are exactly the opposite of the United States. January and February are its hottest summer months.

Large flat plains called pampas cover an area of almost 1,000 miles (1,609 km) in the center of Argentina. The word *pampa* means "level plain." Crops such as wheat, soybeans, sunflowers, and corn are grown here.

As of July 2003, there were 38,740,807 people living in Argentina.

43

Proud to Be Argentine

Jorge Luis Borges (1899 – 1986)

Borges is Argentina's most famous writer. He was born in Buenos Aires and grew up in a home that had a large library of English language books. At fifteen, Borges left Argentina for Europe with his family. He graduated from the high school Collège de Genève in Switzerland. He studied the great European writers and returned to Buenos Aires in 1921. He began to write short stories, poems, and essays. He published his most famous work, *Ficciones* (Fictions), in 1944. From 1955 to 1973, he served as Director of the National Library. When he became blind in 1955, he wrote poems in his head and had someone else write them down.

Evita Perón (1919 – 1952)

Eva Perón, or Evita, was born in poverty in Los Toldos. She dreamed of becoming an actress and moved to Buenos Aires when she was only fifteen years old. Perón got a job as a radio show host. She was able to meet many important people, including her future husband and president of Argentina, Juan Perón. They married in 1945,

and Evita became an important political figure. She worked to secure the right for women to vote in national elections. She was popular with the poor and she encouraged her husband to improve their living conditions. Evita Perón died of cancer in 1952 at the young age of thirty-three.

Gabriela Sabatini (1970–)

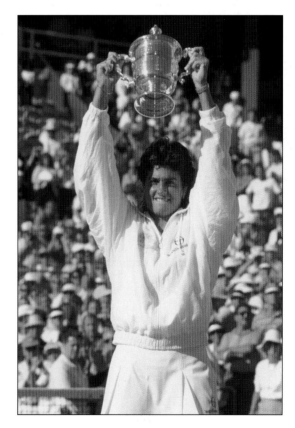

"Gaby" Sabatini was born in Buenos Aires and was the number one tennis player in Argentina and South America. She became a professional at the age of fourteen. She was very popular with fans, both because of her graceful-ness as a player and her great beauty. By the spring of 1992, she had won twenty-five tournaments, including the U.S. Open in 1990. She became one of the world's top tennis players. In 1992, she became the first athlete to have a rose named after her: the Gabriela Sabatini Rose. She shares this honor with people such as President John F. Kennedy and Queen Elizabeth. Sabatini retired from tennis in 1996 at the age of twenty-six.

Find Out More

Books

Countries of the World: Argentina by Nicole Frank. Gareth Stevens Publishing, Wisconsin, 2000.

Enchantment of the World: Argentina by Martin Hintz. Children's Press, Connecticut, 1998.

Nations of the World: Argentina by Anita Dalal. Raintree/Steck-Vaughn Publishers, Texas, 2001.

A True Book: Argentina by Michael Burgan. Children's Press, Connecticut, 1999.

Web Sites*

http://www.surdelsur.com/indexingles.html
A summary of the culture, people, and history of Argentina

http://www.settlement.org/cp/english/argentina
A cultural profile of Argentina

Video

Argentina, Land of Natural Wonders. 1990. VHS, 60 minutes. Video Network.

*All Internet sites were available and accurate when sent to press.

Index

Page numbers for illustrations are in **boldface.**

About the Author

Sharon Gordon has written many nature and science books for young children. She has worked as an advertising copywriter and a book club editor. She is writing other books for the *Discovering Cultures* series. Sharon and her husband Bruce have three teenage children, Douglas, Katie, and Laura, and one spoiled pooch, Samantha. They live in Midland Park, New Jersey. The family especially enjoys traveling to the Outer Banks of North Carolina. After she puts her three children through college, Sharon hopes to visit the many exciting places she has come to love through her writing and research.